School Tools

By Inez Snyder

Children's Press®
A Division of Scholastic Inc.
New York / Toronto / London / Auckland / Sydney
Mexico City / New Delhi / Hong Kong
Danbury, Connecticut

Photo Credits: Cover and all photos by Maura B. McConnell
Contributing Editor: Jennifer Silate
Book Design: Daniel Hosek

Library of Congress Cataloging-in-Publication Data

Snyder, Inez.
School tools / by Inez Snyder.
        p. cm. -- (Tools)
Includes bibliographical references and index.
Summary: Photos and simple text show a young girl using various school tools, including a book
        bag, pencils, and erasers.
    ISBN 0-516-23974-0 (lib. bdg.) -- ISBN 0-516-24039-0 (pbk.)
      1. Schools--Furniture, equipment, etc.--Juvenile literature. [1. Schools.] I. Title.

LB3261 .S69 2002
372.16'7--dc21

                                                                            2001058113

Contents

My name is Robin.

I am going to school today.

4

5

I take my **book bag** to school.

My book bag holds the tools I will use at school.

Class is about to start.

I take my **pencil case** out of my book bag.

9

I keep my **pencils** in my pencil case.

I keep **erasers** in it, too.

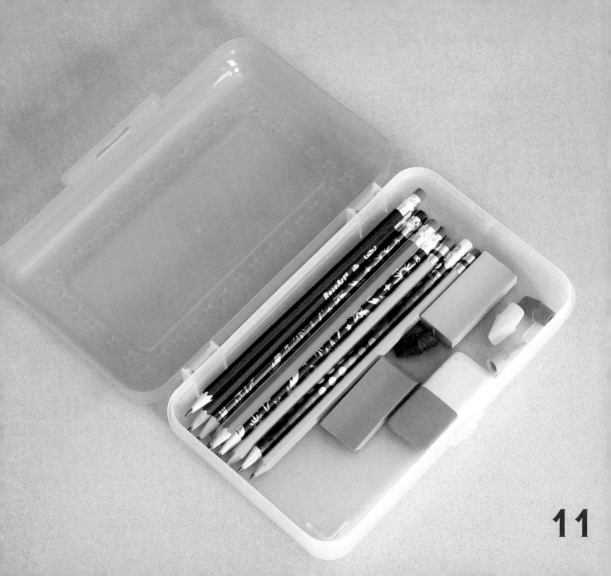

11

I take a pencil from my pencil case.

I will use the pencil to write.

I write in my **notebook** with my pencil.

I write **carefully**.

Sometimes, I make a **mistake** when I write.

I use my eraser to get rid of the mistake.

An eraser takes pencil marks off paper.

I use many tools at school!

20

New Words

book bag (**buk bag**) a sack used for carrying things to school

carefully (**kair**-fuhl-ee) paying close attention when you are doing something

erasers (i-**ray**-surz) things that are used for rubbing off pencil or pen marks from paper

mistake (muh-**stake**) an error

notebook (**noht**-buk) a book of papers for writing in

pencil case (**pen**-suhl **kayss**) a small box or bag that holds pencils and other things

pencils (**pen**-suhlz) tools used for drawing and writing

To Find Out More

Books
The Art Box
by Gail Gibbons
Holiday House

Tools
by Ann Morris
Lothrop, Lee & Shepard Books

Web Site
Fun School
http://www.funschool.com
Play fun games while you learn on this Web site.

Index

About the Author
Inez Snyder writes and edits children's books. She also enjoys painting and cooking for her family.

Reading Consultants
Kris Flynn, Coordinator, Small School District Literacy, The San Diego County Office of Education

Shelly Forys, Certified Reading Recovery Specialist, W.J. Zahnow Elementary School, Waterloo, IL

Sue McAdams, Former President of the North Texas Reading Council of the IRA, and Early Literacy Consultant, Dallas, TX